Bad Boys of Romance History Biographies & Memoirs Seduction Series Volume 1:

Forbidden Seduction Secrets of the Famous and Notable Don Juan

by John Alanis

Table of Contents

Other Revealing Titles by John Alanis

Women Approach You Series Volume 12:

The Dumbest Mistakes Men Make With Women

http://amzn.to/10ktNnR

Women Approach You Series Volume 10:

Wines That Turn Women On

http://amzn.to/11nR1qm

Women Approach You Series Volume 7:
How To Use Words That Turn Women On: Secrets To Sustaining
Attraction
http://amzn.to/RXm25K

See The Complete "Women Approach You" Catalog Here:

http://www.effortlesscommunication.com/amazon/complete-catalog.htm

Important Introduction (Read This First)

You have, doubtless, heard the saying, "those who ignore history are doomed to repeat it." It may be trite, perhaps, but it is also true…and nowhere is their more ignorance of history than in the realm of attraction. Most men are clueless when it comes to not only attracting women, but sustaining that attraction. Yet, when you ask them what books they've read about men who were very attractive to women throughout history, you get blank stares.

Yet there is a LOT to learn from these men, these Bad Boys of History, so to speak. They attracted when in an age when there was no distance media, no birth control, and social repercussions we can't even imagine today. Not only that, they were so attractive, so…infamous, that their names are still well known today. If I say the name "Casanova" or "Don Juan" people immediately know they were great lovers of women, yet they know very little about them, nor have they studied them. That is a crying shame, because the blueprint for attraction is laid out in the history of the lives of these bad boys, especially when you notice similarities in their behavior.

One of the most fascinating and lasting characters is Don Juan. If a man is called a "Don Juan" you immediately know he's good with women, but few men could tell you why. They hear "Don Juan," they think "irresistible to women." But they never ask why.

In this installment of Bad Boys of History, we're going to get into the attractive traits and behaviors of Don Juan, so you can use them in this day and age, and believe me, they work very, very well. Women are dying for men who act like Don Juan. What might surprise you, is his attractive traits aren't what you think. They are actually easy for any man to model, and when you do so in the modern age, the results are amazing.

Attraction really is nothing more than amplifying attractive behaviors, and suppressing unattractive ones, yet few people think like this. But the character of Don Juan did, and that's why he's worth reading about. As you read about him, you'll literally see why he was so attractive to so many women, and how you can adapt his behavior to the modern age. Just be careful not to attract too many women too fast with these secrets!

My name is John Alanis, and for the past 9 years I've taught formerly frustrated men how to succeed with the women they really want, even getting them to approach you first for a date no matter your looks, age or income. I have many happy students who have taken the time to read my material and master the skill of attraction.

I have always been an advocate of reading and studying history. Often you will find someone else has already solved the problems you think are unique, and all you have to do is read about. Human nature is unchanging, especially in the realm of attraction. A few hundred years of civilization have not undone hundreds of thousands of years of evolution, and what Don Juan and other bad boys of history did to attract women works just as well today, as it did back then, probably better. After all, Don Juan didn't have dating sites, social media, even a telephone or car…he'd be a terror in this day and age.

Another reason I read history is because it is enjoyable. Truth is sometimes more entertaining than fiction, especially when it comes to great lovers of history. The more you immerse yourself in history, the more you will learn about present day human nature. I urge you to read this book thoroughly, as well as other volumes in the Bad Boys of History Series. Not only will you enjoy yourself as you read the book, you will enjoy yourself as you use these "forbidden secrets" to attract women in a way few other men ever will.

Let's talk about the bonus material, because I do have a surprise for you. Attraction is as much a visual and auditory process as it is anything else, and while you can certainly learn from words on paper, the best way to do is in conjunction with video. Attraction is a learnable skill, and this book shows you how one man, Don Juan, mastered it. However, there are other things you need to learn, and that's why I've set up a very cool bonus page for you.

On that page are (at least) three videos of me describing and demonstrating vital aspects of attraction, plus links to audios of other books I have recorded. Because you took action and invested in this book, all of these are free for you to access for life. I constantly add new material to this page, so you will want to check back often.

If you click on the link below, you may access the bonus page and those videos. You will get a lot of value from it, and I urge you to watch them either before you read this book, directly after or both. Understanding how attraction really works is vital to your success with women—I do not want to hand you an incomplete work. To access your bonus page, simply click on the link below:

Go To:
www.EffortlessCommunication.com/dj to Access Your Bonus Videos and Mystery Gift

On this page, I have also posted the raw audios I used to create some of my other books about attraction. If you can excuse the occasional four letter word and inappropriate story, you'll get a lot out of them. You can access them by clicking the above link…they are included in addition to your bonus videos.

Whenever I put together a new product, I like to over deliver so…there's even more on the bonus page, much more in fact. Since it is controversial, I cannot reveal what it is in this book (easier explained by video) but when you click on the link to access your bonus video and audios, you will see a video where I explain everything. This "mystery bonus" can suddenly and dramatically change your life with women forever, so I urge you to access it now. You will discover you have gotten far more than your money's worth.

So, welcome aboard. This ebook is the beginning of our relationship, and you'll be hearing more from me in the coming days. Attraction is a complex subject, but not as complex as you might think. Understanding the history of attraction, and reading about all the great lovers and bad boys who came before use will go a long ways toward demystifying it, and when you do so, you will be much more attractive to the women in your life…immediately.

On with the fun…

-John Alanis
The King of Let 'em Come to You

PS I advise you to read through this whole book, preferably multiple times, absorb the information, then start eliminating as many attraction killing behaviors as you can. Don't imitate Don Juan, model his behavior in a way that makes you feel comfortable.

As you may or may not know, men respond to visual stimuli, I have included such stimuli throughout this book: pictures of attractive women. Think of them as motivation. After you read this book (and others I have written) you can go out into the real world and attract women just like this…think about that every time you see a new picture of a hot woman.

Please Be Kind and Review This Book

Forward

So who wants to attract beautiful women at the drop of the hat, any time they want?

You see I'm only asking this because, well, that's why you're reading this book. You're not reading this because you would like to learn about the Don Juan legend or about literary works of Byron for study of English language or Spanish myths and folklore. No, you are reading this specifically because you are a red-blooded man who is completely confused with female behavior and wants to learn how to attract beautiful women. And what better way to learn the art of attraction then by following example of men who came before you and figured it out. Why reinvent the wheel, right?

For anyone else, go buy a book on English romantic literature or take an English class at local community college – this material is not for you.

Section 1: A Strange Question—What Exactly IS Attraction?

What is Attraction?

So let me ask you something – what do you think made Don Juan attractive? Is it the good looks with chiseled physique? Is it the abundance of money, expensive jewelry..? Or is it something else? And if it is something else, how can <u>you</u> obtain it?

Well, I've got good news for you – the attraction is not caused by any of those material things. It is a combination of behaviors and attitudes, and they can be learned. Don Juan had many of the things that I described above but that is not why he was attractive. It was the way he carried himself and the way he behaved that made him the thing of legends.

So what are these "behaviors and attitudes"? Well, if you ever observed a man who's good with women during his interaction with opposite sex, you'll see a few interesting things. First, the woman is almost always laughing and having a good time. Second, he appears in control, looks very comfortable in the setting and on the surface does not look too eager or in rush to go anywhere.

He looks like he is there to just have fun regardless of how things go. If at the end of the evening they part ways so be it, he still had a fun time. If they end up spending the night together, even better – more fun to be had! However, that does not mean he is wishy-washy. He is decisive and is leading the interaction with her in the direction that he wants to go.

Third, he is listening to what she has to say and lets her speak without interrupting as if he's carefully weighing every word coming out of her mouth. She appears more nervous than he is, as if she's the one trying to impress him and not the other way around. So, in a nutshell, the guy has a good sense of humor, is calm and not too eager to impress and satisfy, is in control of the situation and is decisive in his purpose; he is comfortable in the environment that he's in, and is fine with any outcome that happens in the end.

Great! Now you have some idea of what makes a man attractive and you are probably relieved to know that this set of behaviors and attitudes is learnable but as analytical and logical as we guys are, it still does not make sense to us why women are attracted to this type of behavior? So if you want to satisfy your analytical and logical male brain, read on through the next section. If you don't care skip the next section, but you're going to be missing out…

The Purpose of Attraction

Look, I don't know what your personal belief system is and honestly that's none of my business. Whether you believe our ancestors came from the trees as monkeys and evolved into our present form, or whether you believe we came from Adam and Eve after they were chased out of Eden, or if you think that we came from alien spaceships, that is your business.

Either way we are here on this planet and are part of the animal kingdom. And just the same way animals have their mating rituals we humans have our own form of courtship. After all, the females of each species, including our own, have to make some kind of intelligent decision on who the best partner is for mating and raising offspring.

In the same way male deer grow their antlers, and lions grow their mane and practice their roars, we males of the human species developed over the course of many years, certain sets of behaviors that we hoped were going to attract for us the best specimens of the female kind.

Except unlike the lions and deer of the wild, our sets of attractive behaviors got broken along the way as we evolved into suburb and city dwellers and started relying on our nanny states to provide everything to us from shelter and food to security and healthcare. We human males are no longer required to put on a sheep skin over our privates, take a bow and arrow or a spear and go into the wild hunting for food, or protecting our families from the attack of wild animals.

Fortunately (or unfortunately) for us, the hardest decisions most of us make during the day is which route to take from work to home so as not to get stuck in traffic, or which combo meal we are going to buy today from our local BK.

But, let's say for a moment that you do find yourself in the wild, lost, with no water and food and no modern resources to come to your rescue. You have no one to rely on except yourself. What would you do to make sure you survive the ordeal and come out alive and in one piece? Ok, pop-quiz time!

To survive the above ordeal the best course of action is to –

A) Run around in circles crying and panicking, blaming the cruel fate and cursing everyone and everything for getting you into your current predicament until you mercifully either faint from exhaustion, or knock yourself out by running into a tree.

B) Sing latest hits from Train or Maroon 5 at the top of your lungs until someone hears your pathetic wails and comes to your rescue (hopefully before your nipples start to spontaneously lactate); or

C) Stay calm. Accept that you are in bad situation and get comfortable with it – embrace the suck. Keep a sense of humor about the situation that you're in regardless of how hopeless things look. Come up with the best course of action based on the information you currently have and act decisively upon it. Modify the course of action depending on the results you get and any new information that comes your way. Don't despair and make yourself ok with any outcome since you realize that the outcome does not depend solely on you.

Yes, if you selected C you get a gold star. The behaviors and attitudes that are attractive to women are exactly the same ones that will save you if you ever end up in a life or death situation. Don't believe me? Well read a book "Deep Survival" by a gentleman named Laurence Gonzales (I mean it – read it, it's excellent!). He studies dozens of cases where people found themselves in life or death situations, and the difference each time between survival and tragedy were in the attitudes and behaviors.

Those who behaved in the way described under C had the biggest chance of survival while those who refused to accept their situation, panicked, wailed and cursed their fate ended up perishing. So attraction is not just about sleeping around and having fun with hot women. Yes it is all of those things but it is also a nature's way of ensuring that when chips are down the fittest survive and continue to propagate our species. Unlike us men, women know this instinctively and are subconsciously attracted to the behaviors that to them signals a man who will be there to protect them and their offspring in case of an emergency.

So my question at the beginning of this book can now be rephrased as – Who wants to survive a bad situation and come out on top still breathing the air and then going and bedding all the hot women?

After all Mother Nature is a woman and she loves "bad boys" and hates wusses like all other women do. Learning the art of attraction is really important because men who get dumped by Mother Nature don't get to go home and play with their five-finger girlfriends. When she dumps someone, she ends up reusing their molecules for some other purpose like good source of protein for wild animals or as a fertilizer for surrounding trees.

Now back to our subject – who is this man that's been a thing of legend for almost 600 years and what can we learn from him about attracting beautiful women? I mean, even today when people talk about a guy who is good with women they call him a modern-day Don Juan… Surprisingly, the man is not real. Yes, he is a folk legend, a myth that, like today's James Bond, at one time might have been based on an actual person but grew into a life of its own. When it comes to real-life womanizer, you're thinking of Casanova who in fact was a real person. Either way, that does not make him any less of a great example to follow.

The Legend of Don Juan

The legend of Don Juan was first put in print by a writer named Tirso de Molina. Other writers followed but the theme always stayed the same – an "evil" and "immoral" womanizer who is either punished for his wicked ways by going into hell, or in the last moments of his life repents and asks for divine forgiveness. Wow, talk about the social pressure!

I guess every era had its share of girlie-men and pompous fakes who preached and forced their "moral codes" on others. They obviously wanted to make sure no one was having any naughty fun when they couldn't. So I'm not going to talk about those works since obviously they were corrupted by girlie-men.

Instead I am going to show you the work of another bad-boy of his time a poet by the name Lord Byron. (If you don't know who Lord Byron is, look him up on Internet – he was quite an attractive character - women went wild for him). His poem Don Juan was not meant to moralize us to death with pretending that Don Juan was evil or that womanizing is a cardinal sin for which you go to hell – quite the opposite.

Byron wrote his poem in form of "Cantos" (which means sonnets in Italian) over a period of few years mainly to entertain his audience while at the same time mocking the girlie-men of his era. In fact his poem went so much against his time that he had to change publishers since the first one kept trying to censor his work.

Furthermore, in his poem, unlike in other works about Don Juan, the hero is pursued by women instead of him pursuing them. He is attracting rather than chasing.

In his poem Byron describes the life of his hero from his youth through many of the adventures in his life. Don Juan is described as a child of a local nobleman in Spain who had an early propensity for attracting women. He grew up surrounded by women – his mother was a big influence on him and was in charge of discipline and his education. His first conquest was with an older married woman named Donna Julia who knew him since he was 13 years old.

He ends up being seduced by Donna Julia when he is 16 and she 23. The affair is quickly discovered by Julia's husband and as a consequence Don Juan's mother Donna Inez sends him off to travel the world in hope that his behavior will change. During his first sea voyage, the ship encounters a storm and quickly sinks. Juan ends up surviving the sinking and as a sole survivor ends up on islands of Cyclades in Aegean Sea.

There he is discovered by a young woman named Haidee who takes care of him and nurses him to health. She falls in love with him even though she does not speak his language and can't communicate with him. Haidee's father, however, is a pirate and slave trader. Once he finds Juan with his daughter, he captures him and sends him into slavery to Constantinople.

Once there Juan is bought on a slave market by a man named Baba who is a servant to sultan's favorite young wife Gulbayes. Unbeknownst to Juan, Gulbayes noticed him at the slave market and had purchased him hoping to seduce him. She orders him dressed as a woman and housed in the harem. When Juan rebuffs her advances she is enraged and threatens to have him beheaded.

Instead of ending up Gulbayes'es boy toy, proud Juan ends up with another woman from the harem even further enraging the sultana.

Juan barely escapes with his life and joins the Russian army in their conquest against the Turks. His bravery was such at the battle of Ismail that he got noticed by Russian empress Catherine II who immediately, according to the story, starts lusting after him and takes him in to her confidence. During the same battle he saves a young Muslim girl named Leila from being killed and acts as her protector and benefactor.

Catherine II sends Juan as her envoy to Britain where he is introduced to the high society. He becomes acquainted with noble women of the time, Duchess of Fitz-Fulke, Lady Adelaine and young woman by the name of Aurora. All of these women find him extremely attractive and vie for his attention.

So just looking through this brief description of his adventures, what are the main points that come across?

- First notice that in each instance the women are attracted to Juan without him having to assert himself in front of them. He is attracting them by not trying to attract.

- Second, in many instances the women are competing for his attention. It's as if the attention of one woman is a signal enough that Juan is attractive to all women. He also appears very comfortable in female company and does not feel out of place or shy to talk to them. The more he interacts with women, the more his comfort level increases. You get the sense from reading about him that he truly likes and understands women.

- Third, even though he is in many unpleasant situations, Juan seems to find a way to come out on top (pun intended). No matter what situation he is thrown in, he does not give in to despair but perseveres and ends up being better off at the end.

- Fourth – he is "physically attractive" to women but that does not necessarily mean that he is exceptionally good looking or that he has a ripped physique of today's model.

- He lives by his own code. Whether that means that he refuses the advances of a woman he doesn't like as with the above mentioned sultana, or whether he saves a Muslim orphan girl after a battle at Ismail, Juan has a set of principles that he does not diverge from – even if the price for it is losing his life.

- He is not desperate for female attention and does not get overly excited even at the prospect of having an attractive woman spend the night with him. Throughout the story you get the sense that he just goes with the flow and does not try to assert his influence over others while still being very much noticed by opposite sex.

- He is decisive. Once he decides on the course of action he follows it through. If that means going into the battle or escaping from slavery, once he hatches a plan he comes through with it.

- He is interesting to talk to. He has experienced the real world by going out there and living the life of adventure. He is well read but he does not rely on the books to tell him how the world works. He experiences it first hand and lives to tell interesting stories about it.

- He keeps his word. When he makes a commitment to someone he keeps it. Like the orphan girl Leila whom he adopted after the battle of Ismail. Regardless of his travels and his responsibilities, he still takes care of her like he promised he would, and makes sure that she gets good education and is well fed and clothed.

Every one of the above behaviors shows one clear message about this man – he is reliable and will take care of any woman that he ends up with. It doesn't matter what his looks are or what his financial status is – this man is an evolutionary jackpot for any woman lucky enough to end up with him.

Now, let's compare this with a behavior of typical male specimen of our age. And for that I'll use one my favorite girlie-man stories that has recently come out in media – the baseball wuss! You've probably heard and seen several of these pathetic stories in the past few years and it seems that with every baseball season there are more instances of these types of things happening.

The story usually goes like this – a girlie-man male of our species (I'll call him girlie-male since other name is an offense to men everywhere) is at the ballpark with his girlfriend/wife. They are having fun time – he is into the game while she is looking around, maybe reading a book and not particularly paying attention to the action on the field. Suddenly, the baseball is hit hard in their direction. The girlie-male sees the ball heading their way and ducks and runs off without alerting his date, as the ball ends up hitting the poor woman.

Can there be a more pathetic example of poor male behavior than this? Put this in evolutionary context – if he is so scared of a ball that he fails to protect or even alert her to the danger, how in the world is he going to protect her in case they get attacked by a mugger or rapist, or if they're in a wild – a wild animal like a bear or cougar?

He won't – he'll run off leaving her to fend for herself. You know what they say about running away from the bears? – You don't have to run faster than the bear, you just need to run faster than the person next to you.

Naturally, once the poor woman regained consciousness, she quickly dumped the wuss and went off searching for a better man. Good riddance! But here is the good news – the attractive attitudes and behaviors can be learned and even the baseball wuss could learn to, over time, act like a real man and attract women. The price of this learning process is in time and effort that needs to be taken before one sees the results.

If you follow the right examples, study the actions of others who figured out the art of attraction and apply those lessons in real-life interactions with women, you too can accomplish what many men in this day and age only dream of – to be a modern-day Don Juan. So let's get started with the first attraction secret.

Go To:
www.EffortlessCommunication.com/dj to Access Your Bonus Videos and Mystery Gift

Section 2: The Ten Forbidden Attraction Secrets of Don Juan

Secret #1 - Learn to Truly Like Women

You can't be a chef if you don't like tasting food and cooking and you can't be a writer if you don't like the process of writing. In that same way, you can't be an attractive character to women if you don't like women to begin with. And when I say "like" I don't mean simply in the physical way. Yes, you obviously would like to have sex with hot, beautiful women, otherwise you wouldn't be reading this.

What I'm talking about is truly liking the interaction with women; getting to know them, understanding how they think and behave. I'm talking about learning the nuances of their behaviors and even about things that don't make sense to us guys. Why do they like shopping so much, why do they get moody from time to time, why are they saying one thing but meaning something completely different?

Don Juan is always in company of women. Wherever he goes he's surrounded by them. From early age the main influence in his life was his mother who was in charge of his education and of disciplining him. His first conquest was at 16 but the woman he seduced, Donna Julia knew him as early as age 13.

So how do you get to truly enjoy female company?

First step - Spend more time around women, talking and interacting with them. Yes, it sounds simple but most men are afraid to approach and talk to women. They psych themselves out and allow the nervousness and discomfort to get the better of them.

So instead of starting an awkward conversation right off, try this – in your day to day life whenever you see an attractive woman, smile at her or simply say hi. Get her to smile back at you.

Once you get comfortable doing that day in and day out, take it a bit further and start a simple conversation. The goal is not to right away sweep her of her feet but rather to increase your comfort level in interacting with women. It can be any woman, but the ones I found to have the most enjoyable conversations with are baristas at the local coffee shop or waitresses and girls behind the counters at the local restaurants. Look, they spend their entire work day taking orders from all kinds of people including some who are really irate and unpleasant. You talking to them and trying to have a fun conversation might be just the breath of fresh air they need to brighten up an otherwise dull or stressful workday.

When I talk to one of those girls and if I find the conversations enjoyable, I come back to the same place at a later time and interact with them some more. The trick is to keep pushing the envelope as your comfort level rises and as they get to know you. Don't be afraid to push beyond your comfort level. If you feel that you screwed up and offended her, so be it, learn from the interaction and try not to repeat the same mistake with someone else. You can always stop going to that restaurant or coffee shop if you really feel uncomfortable, but chances are she's most likely not going to be working at that place in few months anyways.

It is really amazing what this type of exercise does for your comfort level and how quickly these types of conversations can grow from something innocent to really quite naughty! Besides the nice benefit is that often times these girls hook me up with free food and other goodies. Not a bad thing at all.

Ok, so that's the first step but that will not take you anywhere unless you also learn the second step – actively listening to her. It's really quite simple – stop the urge to open your mouth and instead let her speak. We guys tend to think that yapping about our possessions or about how great and awesome we are is the way to impressing the women. Nothing could be farther from the truth.

Think about the conversation in this way – if you were talking to someone, man or a woman, and they kept talking and talking and yammering about their day and their life and their accomplishments without letting you utter a word, how long would it take for you to just want to walk away and never see this person again? Yes, just like you want to be heard, women too have things to say and they also want to be heard by others. Except they're surrounded by the bozos who don't keep their mouths shut long enough to let them speak.

So be different – start the conversation, make them comfortable to where they want to talk to you and then quiet down and let them speak. Not only will you be different from other men but you will learn things about her that she might not have divulged to others. You'll learn what kind of behaviors attract her and which ones repulse her. You'll learn about her insecurities, dreams, fears, hopes and aspirations, and you'll realize that women, no matter how beautiful and hot they might be are in a nutshell no different than any other human being on this planet. They are nothing to be feared of or be nervous around.

Secret #2 - Be "Physically Attractive" (It's not what you think it is)

When you think of Don Juan, what do you imagine him to look like? Is he tall, handsome with chiseled features? Is he muscular and strong? If you said yes to these descriptions, you are very much mistaken. Here's how Byron describes him in Canto IX:

"Juan was none of these, but slight and slim,
        Blushing and beardless; and yet ne;ertheless
There was something in his turn of limb,
        And still more in his eye, which seem'd to express
That though he look'd one of the Seraphim,
        There lurk'd a man beneath the spirit's dress."

Wow! <u>You mean he was small and scrawny looking!</u> So if Don Juan does not have any of the physical features that we think constitute an attractive man, why are all of these women so attracted to him at the first sight? What gives? Does being skinny and small make you more attractive than being big and buff?

The answer is – it depends… You see, what we men consider to be "physically attractive" and what women consider to be the same, is very much dependent on the point of view. We see an attractive woman with slim, hourglass shape, large breasts, nice, well shaped booty and just like that we are attracted to her.

From woman's point of view, attractiveness of your physique is more dependent on your underlying attitude. Yes, women do like physical attributes of the man – they like the chiseled physique and the sharp lines on man's face but this again comes through in the context of who they judge to be the "alpha-male". The recent study done by researchers showed that women prefer male faces that show the highest level of confidence. Confidence and certainty in man's face signify higher levels of testosterone which means better health and higher virility.

As always, it comes down to evolution and survival of the fittest. Women will subconsciously always choose a man who shows best survival traits even if their outward appearance is not what society would call attractive. Just think of Peter Dinklage in Game of Thrones or Tony Soprano. They are far from what we would call attractive yet women can't resist them and it all comes down to the certainty of their behavior and the confident attitude they exude.

The good news is – confidence is not something that is naturally given, it can be acquired. Testosterone levels are also not something that are out of your control. They can be increased with proper course of action. So what do you need to do to become more confident or to increase your levels of testosterone?

- First, exercise and especially in the morning right after you wake up. Do a combination of intense weight training and high intensity interval cardio or HIIT. The regular workouts will increase your natural testosterone production and will also help you get rid of the nervousness or aggravation that you might experience in your day to day life. You'll find that you are calmer, more focused and able to take on the challenges of your day with more ease.

- Improve your posture – especially using the lower back exercises. The posture is really important. When you think of a confident looking man, do you see him bent or slouched, or do you think of him as standing erect with his chest out and head up high?

- Find things that you are passionate about in life and pursue them as part of your regular day to day activities. Passion is very important in man's life. A passionate man is someone who is extremely attractive to women. Passion signals to women that you have a purpose and goal in life and are not just spending days killing time.

- Keep interacting with women and developing your attractive traits. This comes back to what I already discussed in previous sections – you can't exude confidence if you are not used to, and are not comfortable being around women. Yes, you might look and feel great and have a sense of accomplishment in your life, but all of those things will not account for much if you are not comfortable in the company of women.

When you're passionate about something whether that something is a team sport, a social cause, type of work you do or a hobby that you're pursuing, you tend to immerse yourself in that activity. You get to overcome challenges that are presented to you and get to feel the exhilaration of overcoming those challenges and succeeding in achieving your goals. Nothing instills confidence in a man than those hard-earned victories. They give you the confidence and certainty that you can achieve more than you originally thought you could, and allow you to approach women with a sense of pride and certainty.

So – confidence is in a nutshell a really simple thing to achieve. Work out regularly, find your passion to pursue and keep interacting with women. The attitudes and behaviors of a confident man will come naturally through following these actions.

Secret #3 - Always Embrace the Situation That You're In

This is really important folks. In life you will often times be in situations that will make you less than comfortable. You might be at a party in a crowd full of unknown people, or you might be going through some hard times at your work. You will feel that the situation is out of your control and it might be preoccupying the majority of your thought process. Yes, for us guys it's a very unsettling feeling since we love to be in control of our world.

The most important thing is to not let this feeling of discomfort affect your interactions with women. Just think about it from her point of view – if you as a man can't handle a relatively minor issue at work, or handle being out of your comfort zone at a party, how will you handle something major like dealing with a natural disaster or some other event that could threaten yours and your family's life?

Women can sense this at a very subconscious level. They will get uncomfortable around you and will start losing respect for you as a man. This is a death knell for any relationship. I know this, since I would go through the same thing in my relationships. Traveling to other countries was especially painful for me, especially if I had to leave the confines of hotel or resort.

I would get worried about how to handle the situation - will we get where we're going on time, will we miss the plane, will we get lost if we go out of the resort, how will we find the way back, how do we communicate with the locals and etc and etc... This in turn made me really nervous and in my case when I got upset and nervous I'd first get really quiet and if my girlfriend at the time would try to talk to me or try to get me to relax I would get abrasive. I can't tell you how many trips I spoiled by doing this.

It wasn't until I started learning about attraction from the works of John Alanis and especially Shelley McMurtry that I realized that this is a huge issue with many men. One of the reasons for this is that we men are not comfortable with letting go of the control.

So how do you do that? Well try this -

First realize that there is nothing that you can do about the situation – it's out of your hands. Get comfortable with that notion. Think of it this way, no matter what happens, if you keep calm and don't lose your head, you don't have to worry about your girlfriend leaving you.

So what if you missed a plane when going to a vacation. There are other flights that you can take and in a meantime, you can explore the airport with her and find something interesting to do. Shop around in the stores, take her to lunch at the airport restaurants. Engage her in conversation and try to keep a positive perspective on things. After all, no matter what, you will eventually get onto a next flight – you won't be stuck at that airport forever, but the damage you do to your relationship with your lousy attitude and irritable behavior might last permanently.

So you got lost while walking around in a foreign place. Just calmly assess your situation and if you're not in a dangerous area, go talk to the locals and ask for directions. Practice your lousy skills in speaking a foreign language, I bet that will make her laugh and also take your mind off of stressful situation. Either way, like they say in military – embrace the suck! Again, the only real threat is from you overreacting and spoiling what otherwise could be a really fun time.

Don Juan was in many situations, good or bad. He was a prisoner, a slave, and at one point even had to dress up as a woman and hide in a harem not to get his head cut off by the sultan. Here's how Byron describes his attitude:

"Juan – in this respect, at least, like saints –
        Was all things unto people of all sorts,
And lived contentedly, without complaints,
        In camps, in ships, in cottages, or courts -"

Throughout his adventures he never once despaired or lost his temper in a bad situation. Instead he stayed calm and made the best of it. And so should you.

Secret #4 - Live in the Real World

Think of this as continuation of what I just described above. To be able to accept any situation that you're in you've got to accept the world the way it is. The world is not kind and fair. It does not care if you're a good person, if you work really hard or if you deserve good things to happen to you. Bad things happen to good people all of the time and they will also happen to you too.

Let me give you a few of my experiences in my 36 years of life – I've survived the Bosnian war and ethnic cleansing when I was just 16 years old – my family and I lost everything and had to run away with our bare lives. At 17 while being a refugee I got cancer and nearly died. At 28 I got cancer again and had to go through radiation therapy – I literally glow in dark how much I got irradiated. At 32 I lost my business and had to fight tooth and nail to stave off bankruptcy.

And yet through it all, I survived and thrived. Now I have my health back, I feel excellent, I live in the greatest country on the planet, my family is good and healthy and not only did I not go into bankruptcy, I am now having a different business and I'm making more money and having more joy in life than I ever did.

And yet none of this means that bad things are not going to happen to me again. I am now at double the risk of getting other cancers due to all of the chemo and radiation therapy that I went through. The global economy might collapse tomorrow and my business might go under again even though I'm doing everything in my power not to have that happen. But one thing I know for sure is that through it all, I will come on top and no matter what I will enjoy my life to its fullest.

Don Juan is exactly the same kind of man. Byron described him the best when he described him as:

"…though a lad,
Had seen the world – which is curious sight,
And very much unlike what people write."

The man that accepts the reality and does not sugar coat his experiences is a very attractive man. To a woman he shows himself to be someone who will realistically detect both the opportunities and the dangers and plan and act accordingly. The man who does not accept the realities of the world runs the risk of making a wrong move at the wrong time and getting himself in trouble.

From my experience, that's how my business failed and almost dragged me into bankruptcy. I was so excited to start my first business and so eager to get going that I didn't fully analyze what my competitive advantage is, how my business differs from others or how much money I will need to keep it going if my original financial estimates don't turn out to be correct. Instead, I viewed the whole thing through rose-color glasses and even though my business took off at the beginning, as soon as the recession hit and my profit margins declined, I got a very rude awakening.

Also, another area where this will definitely bite you if you disregard the realities around you is in attracting the wrong type of woman. Just like there are bad, cruel and deceitful men out there, there are also the same types of women. For example do you know that 1 in 25 Americans (men and women) is a sociopath with no feelings of remorse and no feelings of guilt or responsibility to other people? That's really scary, isn't it?

These women will do everything to present themselves as if they're perfectly normal, well-adjusted individuals while inside they might be out to take advantage of you, hurt you emotionally and physically, and really ruin your life. Just look at Jodi Arias case – she planned and executed the murder of her boyfriend at a time, by stabbing him 29 times! How insane is that?!

You can always spot these individuals if you pay attention to what's really in front of you and not get drawn in into the web of attraction. Yes, it is a great feeling to have a woman who appears to be into you, but always make sure you step out of the feeling of attraction and look at the relationship and at her in realistic way. If you notice any of her behaviors or actions that disturb you, don't try and justify them but rather focus on what they truly mean. You just might save yourself from a lot of heartbreak and pain.

So look at things in the world the way they really are and not what you would want them to be. Is it uncomfortable? – Yes. Does it make you take off your rose-colored glasses and stop looking at the pretty view you want to see? – Yes. But in the end the final view you get is much more pleasant than anything your mind can come up with.

Secret #5 - Be a Genuine Article (Don't Be a Pretender)

What do I mean by that? Well, don't pretend to be someone that you're not. Don't be a fake. The world is filled with people who talk to make themselves feel good. They go on and on about how they will do this and that in their life but never end up actually doing anything to give substance to their words.

I have a couple of friends who talk about running a marathon and come to me for advice since I already ran two. They ask questions, do research on proper training and nutrition and even start a workout regimen… for about 2-3 days and then all of their plans fall by the waist side. The marathon date comes and they do what they have done for the last 3 or 4 years since they got the idea of running a marathon in their heads – they stay home.

Sure enough, as soon as the next marathon is advertised, the whole process continues. I often wondered why someone would open their yapper and talk and talk but never actually come through with their plans. Is it that they try to make themselves feel good? Is it that they feel that talking is the same as doing something? I don't know – I never had that attitude so I can't tell. But one thing that this behavior does show to me is the level of laziness that is prevalent in our society.

Just a few days ago I came across a website called MoveOn.org. Supposedly it is a site that strives to change the world for the better by taking action to improve people's lives from helping students with student debt to helping immigrant families toward the path to citizenship and many other, in my opinion, worthwhile causes. Except – they aren't really doing anything – the whole purpose of the site is to start and sign petitions. Yes, that's all of the progressive action they take. You can sit on your butt and without getting out of the chair, start or sign a petition for a cause.

Does that help anyone get rid of the student debt? Do immigrant families still have issues with immigration laws? Are there still hungry and homeless people out there who need help? Yes, and all these petition clowns do is sit on their rear ends and type their names into the web page. I'm sure a starving person feels so much better now that you wrote your name on some web page. Oh, no, wait, they are still starving!

This is symptomatic of our entire society now. Where before people would join Peace Corps or Habitat for Humanity and actually go and build houses, deliver food and medicine and actually make difference in the real world, today's generation is more content with sitting and staring at the computer.

And this is not even the worst of it. These days people can sit behind their computers and assume whole new fake identities for themselves and start living in the virtual worlds. Sites like SecondLife.com and MyVirtualLife.com offer users an escape from their boring existence by creating a brand new online persona. It's an addiction and a form of self-delusion that really doesn't do anything more for you than make you even more inept at face-to-face interactions.

Don Juan is not a fake. In every one of the descriptions of him and his character he does what he says he will even if that action will cause him a great bodily harm or death. He refuses to indulge the whim of a very powerful woman (sultana) knowing that he might face death. When he decides to escape he does so when the chance presents itself. When he is with the Russian army at Ismail, he fights bravely and when he rescues an orphan girl, he does take care of her like he committed himself.

So follow his example. Don't talk about or make commitments to things that you're not sure you'll be able to accomplish. If you do, make it a point to come through with your actions no matter how hard things get. I know from my own experience that when I commit to something, the pain of not holding up to my end of the bargain is such that it pales in comparison to the inconvenience and pain of action. Having that attitude is key to becoming a genuinely trustworthy man.

So how does this relate to attraction? Simple, if a woman can't trust you when you commit to something, she can't trust that you will be there to provide for her or her child. Without strong sense of commitment, you've just relegated yourself to the evolutionary dumpster.

Secret #6 - Live by Your Own Code

Let me ask you this? What do you stand for as a man? Think about it for a minute. What is it that defines you as you – what are your goals, your life philosophy, your attitudes toward life? Most men don't think about this and instead spend their days muddling around aimlessly through their lives. They wake up every day, go to their jobs, come back home in the evening and then sit around aimlessly watching TV shows until it's time to go to bed. They might spend time with their friends or have a BBQ over the weekend but that's the extent of their involvement in other activities.

What do you think life with that man is like? It's really, really, really boring. That man brings nothing new to the relationship, has no direction in which to take his life, no goals or aspirations and no vision for his future besides what game to watch on TV or which fast food joint to visit. To me that is a sad, pointless existence especially in a country like the US where there are so many possibilities and so many opportunities.

So think real hard about the above question. What do you stand for and what direction is your life going in?

As your thinking about this question, do this – pull out a piece of paper and write at least ten attributes that describe you. Are you thoughtful, fit, trustworthy, knowledgeable, intelligent and etc.? Don't stop at ten, keep going – the more you write the more you'll get to know yourself. Once you finished writing it, read it out aloud and really think of some examples where you truly showed those features.

Then beside it or under it write at least ten attributes that you would like to have. Be as specific as possible. Do you wish to be more courageous, more confident, less nervous around women, less irritable when in new environment, or more active? Once you write down that list, read it aloud and think about course of action you can take to improve yourself.

I did this myself few years back and when I read out aloud the list of things I wanted to improve certain things started to click. In my case, I was finding that I have a lot of fears that I wanted to get rid of. For example my list of improvements included:

- Being more courageous when faced with aggressive people,

- Lose my fear of heights

- Lose my fear of airplanes and flying

So after I looked over the list I came up with a list of actions that I needed to take to get over all these fears. To get courage to stand up for myself, I started taking kickboxing and MMA classes. Yes, it was a very scary and very unpleasant process but even though I did not like to be in a ring sparring and getting my face and body pummeled, I kept at it for year and a half until I felt that I had sufficient enough of a skill to protect myself. I made a promise to myself that I will always try and avoid confrontation unless I have no other available choice and at that point I will take all of my knowledge and defend myself to the end. That became one of the things I stand for in my life.

To lose my fear of heights, I joined the local rock climbing gym and started going regularly. There I met a lot of fun people who helped me with advice and pushed me to get better at climbing and less concerned with the heights aspect of it. Eventually I started climbing multi-pitch 200-300 ft. walls in the outdoors. I even took up ice climbing over the winter and discovered that I have a real appetite for that type of adventure. Having adventures like rock and ice climbing also became something that I live for.

To lose my fear of flying I took flying lessons. I can't tell you the amount of exhilaration and pride I felt when I first took off with a plane without the help of my instructor. It was one of the most exciting things I've ever done in my life and the excitement of it lasted for whole of 2.5 seconds until a gust of wind forced the plane to sharply bank on the left side. I tell you, if I didn't get a heart attack at that moment, I never will. Pushing myself out of my comfort zone and facing my fears also became something I stand for in my life.

So, think about this and write down your lists and start working on improving your life.

Secret #7 - Have Interesting Stories to Tell

This is by far my favorite attraction secret! Mostly because over the years I made myself into a good storyteller. I can't tell you how many times I would tell a story from my experience to a female acquaintance and then just watched as her eyes would light up. It was as if I could tell the exact time when the attraction switch would go off in their heads. The only thing missing at that moment would be the soundtrack of the choir singing "Hallelujah" in the background. Man, after that they would look at me in a completely different way.

You see women love good story tellers. Men who are able to tell stories in interesting way are extremely attractive since good storytelling truly engages woman's mind. It also shows you to be a person of high intelligence, someone who is creative, experienced and exciting – unfortunately not a regular male most women interact with day to day.

Don Juan, even though he was young, was a great storyteller. Listen to how Byron describes him:

"But Juan was a bachelor – of arts,
     And parts, and hearts: he danced and sung, …

…

     …and could be sad
Or cheerful, without any "flaws of starts,"
     Just at the proper time; and though a lad,
Had seen the world – which is curious sight,
And very much unlike what people write."

Basically Juan was an intelligent and educated man who was able to engage people's hearts through his stories. He could switch between the emotions from sadness to cheerfulness just at the right moment in the story to keep the listener interested. Even though he was young and looked inexperienced he would surprise his listeners by talking about his real life experiences. Talk about adding authenticity to your stories!

So how can you get to become a great storyteller? It's really not a complicated process but it requires work:

- First and most basic step is to have something to talk about. Look – think about events in your life and your experiences. What made them interesting, funny, sad, heartbreaking, unusual or downright weird? If you were listening to someone else talk about events from your life, as if they were their own, would you be interested in listening? If not then are there any new experiences or things you could do in your life that will make it more interesting? Can you take up a new hobby or go travel to some interesting destination?

- Use descriptive language. It doesn't matter if the subject of you story is the most amazing in the history of human experiences. If you don't describe it in an interesting way, your story is wasted on the listener. So when telling a story find ways to use descriptive language. Describe the events so as to make your listener feel that they are right then and there as the story is happening.

- Mix different emotions in your story. You might be describing a funny event that happened to you but try and see if you can add a bit of a serious note to it. Alternatively, if you're talking about a serious event, infuse your story with humor. This keeps your audience engaged and shows them that you're neither an immature clown nor somebody who takes themselves too seriously.

- Prepare ahead of time. I know it sounds kind of weird but what always worked for me was to think of a few interesting events from my life and tell a story about them in my head and mentally rehearse it as if I were telling it to a group of people. I'd go over it multiple times in my mind and each time try to make a change to improve it. I'd try and visualize myself telling it to a group of women and visualize the reaction of the audience - what reaction would I like to see. Then I would make a mental note of the story so that I can tell it at the right time when it becomes relevant to the group conversation. This method works wonders because it makes me look spontaneous yet interesting. As the saying goes – I can be spontaneous if I practice few hours every day.

Now there's a caveat to all of this and that's – don't make things up. If you don't know much about a certain subject or you have not experienced something, then don't talk about it. You'll sound disingenuous at best and as a liar at the worst. That is not an impression you want to leave on a woman.

There's one other big factor in making yourself a good storyteller – you've got to live in the real world. Not the world of should be's and could be's but the world as it really is, and then inject that real world experience into your stories. Don't sugar-coat your experiences or use political correctness.

For example, if you're telling a story of how you made a fool of yourself, then tell it the way it happened and admit that you did in fact act or look like an idiot. If you're telling the story that involves profane language, either use that language or don't tell that story to begin with. Again, not doing this will make you look like a fake or like someone who's trying too hard to be liked.

Secret #8 - Use Your Touch to Create Sexual Tension

In Canto I of Don Juan where Juan interacts with Donna Julia, there is a great description of how a touch when properly done can be used to create sexual tension with a woman. Check out this verse where Byron describes the touch of the hand that:

"Withdrew itself but left behind
      A little pressure, thrilling, and so bland
And slight, so very slight, that to the mind
      'Twas but a doubt; but ne'er magician's wand"

Folks, touch can be a great way to create sexual tension with a woman. While we men react to sexual stimuli as an on/off switch, women react differently. Their sexual stimulation is like a spring that needs to be wound slowly before it, well, springs into action. Do it too fast and you risk damaging it.

Imagine this situation - you're talking to a woman and having a good time. The conversation is going great and she looks like she really likes you. All of a sudden, you reach out and out of nowhere you grab her by her arm and squeeze her. Chances are she's not going to like that even if your intentions were to just get a little closer to her.

Why? – Well, for one it makes her feel like you're behaving erratically and might be aiming to physically hurt her. At the least, it makes her feel that you have a lousy impulse control and no woman wants to be around man like that. Evolution has taught woman that man with lousy impulse control eventually end up hurting them or even killing them.

Now, let's go back to the same situation but instead of initializing any type of contact with her, you just stand there keeping your distance no matter how much the conversation is going in the right direction. What will she think of you then? Well, at best she might think that you're not really interested in her and leave. At worst she might think of you as a timid wuss who is too afraid to make a move even when the obvious opportunity presents itself in front of him. Ouch! Not a good place to be either.

Remember our discussion on evolution and natural selection and what role attraction plays in it? Well if we put your behavior in that context, you are either a potential abuser who can't control his behavior and will end up hurting or killing her and her offspring, or you are a weakling who is too afraid to act in front of a woman who likes him, let alone stand strong in front of other men if they try to hurt her. Either way you showed yourself to be an evolutionary dead end to her, and she'll likely move on to a calmer and stronger man.

So what is the proper way to behave in this situation? Well just like Byron described in Don Juan, use slight touch or a slight squeeze at a proper moment and then retreat leaving her wanting more. Think about the same interaction with a woman that we just described above. Instead of suddenly reaching for her, or not touching her at all, wait for a moment where she laughs at your joke or smiles at you and gently touch her on the back of her hand or on her knee if you are sitting facing each other.

The key is to make it a quick and gentle touch and then retreat. You just initialized a contact and have made her more comfortable with you. On top of that you just made her wonder if you really like her or if you are just friends. You're also timing your touch so as to create an association between a pleasant feeling (happiness, joy) and your touch.

Secret #9 - Don't Try too Hard

Listen, I know - I've been there. You meet a girl that you find really attractive and you are so desperate to make her like you, that you will do anything, say anything to get her. Except whatever you try to do, it never seems to work in your favor. It's frustrating, it drives you nutz, it sucks...

The simple truth is that most of the time, there is nothing that you can do to make someone attracted to you. You can learn all of the attraction secrets, be confident, interesting, and say and do things in just the right way, and you're still not guaranteed that a woman will in fact be attracted to you.

That's just the way things are. So the secret is that to truly attract women you must not focus so hard on trying to attract them. Here's what Byron said of Don Juan:

"His manner was perhaps the more seductive,
          Because he ne'er seem'd anxious to seduce;
Nothing affected, studied or constructive
          Of *coxcombry* (pretentiousness) or conquest; no abuse…"

Juan attracted by not attracting. What that really means is that he kept his composure when surrounded by beautiful women and kept true to himself. He did not let woman's beauty take over his thought process and instead he stayed focused on what he wanted.

Recent study by Canadian researchers discovered that exposure to beautiful women temporarily lowers down male IQ especially in the areas of reasoning and comprehension. What it means is that when a man sees a beautiful woman, his natural instinct kicks in and overrides his thought process. Basically our sexual attraction to them makes us guys temporarily stupid.

As a result most of us end up either overreacting to this feeling of attraction and try to force the woman to like us by showing off and bragging, or our minds just short-circuit and we find ourselves not being able to speak or act. As a result we either come across as too pushy and a bit threatening, or as awkward and week.

Again, coming back to evolution, remember what that signals to a woman – if you're too pushy she feels that she can't trust you. After all what will happen if she doesn't do what you want her to do? She's subconsciously considering if you'll get violent with her or try to force yourself on her. Alternatively, if you are unable to act in front of her, how are you going to handle yourself in a real threat? Will you freeze, crumble, whimper?

Besides, all of these behaviors signal to a woman that you are attracted to her and that she can have you any time she wants. There is no thrill of seduction, there is no wandering in her mind if you like her or not. Just the same way we guys are attracted to a woman's pretty face, nice legs and well-shaped curves, the women are attracted on a mental level to the feeling of chase and excitement of not knowing if you like her or not.

Imagine a heavy-set, obnoxious woman – would you be attracted to her? Probably not. Well, the guy who is too eager and tries too hard is a sort of a "heavy-set, obnoxious woman" equivalent to a woman. Now imaging a woman with ugly facial features, bad teeth and skin, no curves, and with just overall unhealthy look. Would you be attracted to her? Again – no. Well if you freeze in front of the woman and let her beauty take over your thought process, you are basically becoming that unhealthy looking chick to her.

Think about it from their perspective. Here she is, blessed by good looks, having all of the features that men find attractive and yet can't get a man who can make her feel the feeling of attraction. Instead, she either never gets approached or when she does, the guy either acts like a blabbering, overexcited idiot, or freezes and awkwardly mumbles words to her. Kind of a sad thing if you think about it, right? Don't you think she deserves better than that? Help the poor girl out by becoming the man she really wants.

So what's the key to overcoming these urges to either try too hard or to freeze up when talking to a woman? Well, first let me tell you a story from my own experience. I grew up in a small town where most people knew each other. My 2nd cousin from my dad's side was one of the most beautiful girls in our town. She was a few years older than me and I spent a lot of time hanging around her. I noticed a lot of guys try to talk to her and try to get her attention or get just downright smitten when coming face to face with her. It never made sense to me since I knew her so well and she didn't seem intimidating. She was just my cousin and a friend and no different than any other friend I hung out with.

So basically the key is to get comfortable being around beautiful women by spending more time around them. And how do you do that? Well, it goes to the previous lesson of learning to truly like women. Start first by giving them a smile and see if they smile back. Once you're comfortable doing that, start a simple conversation. Yes, you'll be nervous at first and you will appear either too eager if you see that she's responding positively to you, or you'll kind of come across weird and skittish if you see that the conversation is not going the way you want it to.

Yes, I've been there, it is a very uncomfortable feeling but it is just a feeling and it's not going to kill you. In all my experience I have never seen a guy approach a woman to just try and talk to her and have her in turn jump on him, bite his neck and rip his throat out leaving him convalescing in a pool of his blood. It never happens!

She might turn you down, she might walk away annoyed, or maybe even offended - who knows…? But trust me you'll still be breathing the air after the whole thing is done and the only residual thing you'll have is a feeling of embarrassment that will soon pass. Push past that discomfort and try with some other woman if this one bombs out on you.

The key is to get more and more comfortable with each interaction. Notice things that you're doing that either create or destroy her interest in you and make a mental note of them for future. Basically focus more on the process rather than the outcome. What does that mean? Well, focus more on what you're doing and try to avoid doing wrong things. Only focus on her reactions as a sort of an indicator on whether or not you're doing the right things.

Over time, as you get more comfortable around beautiful women, you'll see that their influence on your thought process and emotions will fade. Just like getting used to anything else, the novel effect of being around them will eventually wear off. At that point, you'll be more capable of controlling the interaction with them and you'll start becoming something that very few men these days are – a truly attractive character.

Secret #10 - Be Decisive – Make Your Move When Time is Right

Here is one analogy that might be helpful in understanding this secret. Let's say you're in the process of buying a new car. You go from dealer to dealer and you're neither finding the car you want nor the salesman who makes you feel comfortable. Then you go into a new lot and find a car that interests you. The salesman approaches you and at first sight he looks professional, does not appear to be too eager to sell you just anything, and his whole demeanor and the way he explains the features of the car make you feel very comfortable.

He slowly gains your trust. You can see that he cares about your satisfaction with the purchase process and the vehicle and is not just there to sell you just anything. You are more and more excited about the prospect of buying the car. He comes back and gets your financial information and starts you on the credit approval process. And then as the process is done and you're ready to sign the papers and get the keys, he just goes away and leaves you waiting.

You would not be happy with that at all. All of this time and anticipation, hard work from his side and thought process on yours and all for nothing. Kind of frustrating isn't it? And that's exactly how a woman feels if you do all of the things right in the attraction process but don't make your move when the time is right.

It would give anyone a weird and unsettling feeling. Think about it – wouldn't you feel that there was something wrong with you if that happened to you? Not being decisive and going for it is a sure fire way to kill all of your chances with her.

When you look at the example of Don Juan, he never seemed to have the issue with acting even when he wasn't sure of what effect his actions will have. And that's the key thing, no matter what you do, taking action always beats doing nothing, even if that action turns out to be wrong. I think it's Teddy Roosevelt who said:

"In any situation, the best thing to do is to do the right thing. The next best thing to do is the wrong thing. The worst thing to do is nothing."

We guys are analytical creatures. Our male brains will analyze our environment and try to process what's happening around us and give it a meaning. When in the company of a beautiful woman, especially as you're first learning the art of attraction, your brain will tend to over analyze every word she says and every gesture that she makes, looking for the right moment to act. If you let yourself fall into trap of overanalyzing every gesture, you will end up basically paralyzing yourself into inaction. What's the term? – "Paralysis through over-analysis."

So look, unless you all of a sudden develop telepathic powers, you will never be able to tell for sure when a woman is ready for you to make a move. And it also depends from woman to woman. Some will give you subtle hints while others will make it more obvious to you, but either way, it should always be up to you when to act. Yes, analyze your interaction with her. Yes, look for clues that she's ready, but have a threshold of when you think it is obviously your turn to act and just go for it.

The worst thing that can happen is you misread the signals and get turned down. Oh well, big deal! You're still alive and breathing, the sun will still come up tomorrow and the world will not end. And yes, you learn the lesson and get to try again. And besides, sometimes women will turn you down just to see if you're persistent enough to try again.

Go To:
www.EffortlessCommunication.com/dj to Access Your Bonus Videos and Mystery Gift

Section 3: How to Use Don Juan's Devastatingly Effective Attraction Secrets to Attract the Women You Desire- the Step by Step Formula Revealed

The Next Steps

Now that we've gone through the main attraction secrets of Don Juan, let's talk about how to put together a plan of action and what to expect as you're mastering these attraction skills.

Yes it's quite a lot of things to consider but at least what I hope that you got from the above sections is that attraction is a learnable skill and that Don Juan was no more physically advantageous than you are. You can learn this stuff but again, the price that you will have to pay is in time spent and in actions that you need to take.

So now that you read the above secrets, let me put a very usual scenario in front of you and see what you could do differently.

Imagine this – a man is meeting a woman for the first time. It's their first date. He's at a bar or a restaurant waiting for her to arrive. He checks himself to make sure he doesn't stink and that he looks clean. He's nervous and his palms are sweaty. He's rehearsing in his head what to say and hopes that she will like his jokes and will be impressed by his stories about his job, or his pet, or his last vacation. How do you think this evening is going to go for him?

Well if you paid attention to any of the above lessons, you know that this is a recipe for a disaster. This guy should get ready to go back home and cry himself to sleep hugging his pillow. Sorry, you're not getting any this time butch.

Now, applying the lessons from above, what are some of the things that you could do better in this situation? Let's go through them together.

Action Item #1 – Destroy Your Fears

This book is about attracting women. It's not about hunting tigers or jumping out of airplanes or getting into a fight with an MMA fighter. No physical harm will come to you out of interacting with women. So realistically speaking, what exactly are you afraid of? Are you scared of embarrassment? Maybe rejection? Feeling of being sexually inadequate? Maybe deep down you're scared that you will never find the right person and will stay forever lonely?

Understand this, yes there might be unpleasant, awkward and down-right embarrassing moments in your quest to master attraction. Yes, you will most likely get rejected many, many times. And yes, it will suck coming back home after being rejected and feeling lonely. I know that – I've been through that myself. But also know this too - any emotional "damage" you experience because of these events is a result of you not mentally preparing yourself enough and realizing that bad emotions are just that – emotions that will go away in few hours.

So how do you get over your fears especially when first starting to learn attraction? Here are some simple steps that worked for me:

- Don't go on dates – Yes, I hate the 'D'-word. It implies going to some restaurant or noisy bar and trying to impress each other. You're both nervous and the conversation can't flow normally. The pressure is palpable and just the overall vibe of the whole thing is unpleasant.

- Instead, ask her to meet up for a coffee or a few drinks right after work and keep it short. Tell her you're really busy and have plenty of important things to do so you can only hang out for an hour or so. That way if things go bad you already have an escape plan, and if things work out, well I guess you can always do those "important things" at some other time. It's not a date just an informal get-together. This will keep your interaction relaxed and remove all of that "date" pressure off of your back.

- If things don't go your way and you end up feeling alone and rejected, turn those feelings on their head. What really worked for me is I would always come up with reasons and examples of how lame or uninteresting she was to me. That would stop me from focusing on myself and from thinking of myself as a failure.

- If you say or do something that she doesn't like, if you get embarrassed by something, or if for whatever reason, things between you and her get weird or unpleasant, don't focus on that emotion and don't let it paralyze you from trying again with someone else. What really worked for me is I would use that bad date as a funny story that I could tell a group of friends and have a laugh about it. Yes, I would embellish and exaggerate the events but the purpose behind it is to change my mindset from focusing on failure.

All of these steps might sound to you as a form of self-delusion, but they are not. What you're basically doing is making yourself realize that all of these things that you're going through are just temporary growing pains and that you are not going to let these setbacks affect you on your ultimate quest. This is a very realistic view of things and has nothing to do with deluding yourself.

Action Item #2 – Determine What You Want in a Woman

Just like you don't take a road trip if you don't know where you want to go, you don't start the process of learning attraction if you don't really know what type of woman you want to attract in the first place. Otherwise you run a risk of attracting women who are just not your type while missing out on somebody whose company and attention you would really enjoy.

The simplest way you can figure out what exactly you're looking for in a women is to make a list of at least 10 physical and personality traits that you find attractive in a woman. It can be more than 10 items but as a rule make it at least 10. Do you want her to be slim, blonde, black-haired or tall? Do you want her to have a great sense of humor, be well educated, be career oriented, or do you want her to be more laid back and relaxed? What kind of interest or hobbies do you imagine her to have – is she into dancing, outdoors activities or is she more of a home body.

Either way once you do this, you'll have a better idea of what type of person you want and you'll also have a better idea where to go to meet that type of a woman. If you want someone who's into dancing then take couple of dance classes. If you want someone who's outdoorsy, join a rock climbing gym or some type of a mountaineering society.

Also, as you hang around more women and you get more and more experience in interacting with them, you might find that your idea of what you want from a woman changes. You might find that you don't enjoy certain things and that instead you want somebody with a different set of qualities than what you originally thought.

In my case, I used to think that I like Latin girls, so I dated a few and figured out that they are just not my type. Instead I found out that I'm more attracted to Eastern European and middle-eastern women. I also thought that I liked a home-body but after being with one, I decided that my life is better spent with somebody who's more outdoorsy. My preferences just changed with time. And with it the action that I took to meet the right type of woman for me, also changed.

Action Item #3 – Divide Large Task into Small Steps

Yes all of this might seem daunting to you since there is just so much stuff to learn and memorize. But here is the trick to mastering it – divide and conquer. Simply divide the task at hand into smaller steps and execute each step separately. I'm a software developer and small businessman by profession so throughout my day I have a large number of tasks to perform and execute. Some of these tasks are really immense. There are so many times when I look at the size of my workload and I just feel like throwing in a towel and heading home.

For example, I might be tasked with developing an e-commerce website for a certain company that together with processing customer orders also handles customer complaints, customer correspondence and also reports data to company managers. This is a huge project, but my first thought whenever I am faced with something of that magnitude is how to divide it into smaller pieces that then fit together.

I might complete one small programming module, test it and get it to work. Right there I've just accomplished a small step toward project completion. Then I complete another web page and then another. Soon enough I have sizable system that has many of the features working. That gives me confidence and drive to continue on.

Same goes with tackling the mastery of attraction. Focus on one thing that you know you're not good at. It might be that you're not spending enough time around beautiful women. Or it might be how you're uncomfortable starting a conversation, and then take small steps toward improving your skill. Remember what I said earlier about getting yourself to be more comfortable talking to women – take small steps, start smiling at them, have them return a smile back, then start a simple conversation and etc.

Each time you succeed and get better at a certain aspect of attraction, celebrate that success as a small victory. That kind of attitude will make you more willing to take further steps and continue to improve.

Action Item #4 – Adjust Your Approach Depending on Her Preference

Just in the same way that no two people have the same sets of fingerprints, no two individuals communicate in the same way. Yes, the attraction secrets that were out lined in the above chapters will work for many women but the way you approach and communicate with each individual woman will vary depending on how she likes to interact.

You've got to adjust your communication style to individual person otherwise your message is not going to get heard. What does that mean – if she's more talkative than you, let her speak and don't jump into her sentence. If she's more inclined to listen, then make sure you have things to talk about.

Also, people tend to like others who talk in the same way as they do. The fast talker will look down on a slow talker and consider them dumb while a slow talker might be annoyed with the speed of words coming from fast talker's mouth. People who talk loudly tend to like other individuals who do the same thing, and vice versa.

So pay attention to the way she talks, the tone and volume of her voice, and the speed at which she speaks and try and reproduce it. Also notice what types of conversations are acceptable to her and which ones are not. Is she offended by certain subjects? Are certain subjects off limit, or is she comfortable with any conversation? Does she use occasional profanity in her speech or is she offended by it?

Adjusting your style of communication will help you gain person's respect. This is something that's not just limited to women. The better you are at it and the more closely you pay attention to person's communication patterns, the more influence and trust you'll gain from them. And, as you already know, you can't go anywhere in the attraction process without first gaining a woman's trust and respect.

Action Item #5 - Don't Give Up at the First 'No'

Just like any type of skill, attraction takes time to master. You'll spend time around women and you'll get better and better at interacting with them but you'll still have to make your move and close the deal, at which point you'll hear a word 'no' quite a lot. Yes, the scariest word in English language, the word that stops average men in their tracks. Yes, we've all been conditioned by the media girlie-men (or "she men" like Byron called them in Don Juan) squealing about how 'no' is a sure fire signal to stop and give up.

There are so many negative connotations that have over time gotten associated with this word that whole books have been written about it. Let's just think of all things that word 'no' means to most people these days:

- You've failed
- You've been rejected
- You're not worthy
- You should give up
- You should stop
- Do not bother
- Don't be annoying

The successful man is, however, not intimidated by the word 'no'. Let's see what word 'no' really means to a successful person (whether that person is successful in business, successful with women or any other area of life).

- You're close
- You need to try again

- You need to modify your approach
- You need to ask in a different way
- You're almost there

Big difference isn't it? So back to our original example – you've just heard a 'no' from a woman. What should you do? Do you whimper away with a tail between your legs? Do you get upset and start arguing with her to try and make her see your point? Of course not.

Again, remember the evolution and what those actions say to a woman – that in first case you're a weakling that can be chased away and discouraged by slightest threat or obstacle, and in the second case you're showing yourself to be an unstable, aggressive and scary person that might end up eventually hurting her if he doesn't get his way.

Here's a little secret that you should know – when a woman says 'no' if she really means it, you'll never see her again. She will just stop seeing you – full stop. Otherwise, if she says 'no' but continues to hang out with you, it's a signal for you to try a different approach, ask questions in a different way, use your attractive character even more and get her to eventually say 'yes'. One of my business associates used to call this kind of thinking as "Gentle Pressure Applied with Incredible Persistence".

A man who can keep his attractive character and not be dissuaded by the initial rejection is the man who shows intelligence, perseverance and strength of character. It's also quite flattering to a woman that a man cares enough and is focused enough on her to keep trying to seduce her. This behavior signals to her that she's dealing with the man she can truly rely on and who won't leave her at the time of need.

Action Item #6 – Focus More on Avoiding Mistakes

Attraction is a really weird process. You can do everything right, say and do all the right things, be charming, a "bad boy", show yourself as an "alpha-male", take decisive action and etc., but if at any point you make a mistake, all of that hard work is for nothing. In one of the above sections I mentioned that some attraction secrets are so powerful that when used properly you can almost tell the exact moment the girl feels the attraction toward you.

Well, in the same way, most mistakes in the attraction process are also powerful enough to where you can almost tell when the glimmer of attraction and excitement dies in her eyes. From talking to my female friends, I hear so many stories of them meeting bozos, fakes, pretenders, whiners, complainers, cry-babies and downright creepy guys that they feel so frustrated with a whole dating process.

So think about it from their perspective – you meet them, show them your attractive character and they get a feeling of attraction and hope that they have finally found in you a man who truly is worth their attention. Everything is going great and then you do or say something unattractive that brings the whole process to a grinding halt. All of the sudden her hope is shattered and she can't help but feel tricked and cheated by you. Just as she thought she found the real man, he turns out to be a pretender. She doesn't know or care that you're just developing your attractive character, she just knows that you're no different than any other "she man" out there.

If the roles were reversed, wouldn't you feel kind of the same? So while making a mistake is nothing to fear and is definitely not something that should stop you from acting since yes, you will make mistakes during the learning process, you have to understand why your mistakes have such an ill effect on the whole attraction process.

So the key to getting better in learning attraction is to not only learn and adopt attractive behavior but to also be aware of your unattractive behaviors and suppress them. The simplest way of doing that is to take above attraction secrets and compare them against your behaviors. And be brutally honest with yourself - Do you get upset at the wrong times? Do you whine and complain in situations when you should be calm and collected? Do you tend to get nervous when talking to a woman for the first time? Whatever these behaviors are, write them down and make yourself aware of them. Then make a plan of action on how to avoid them in the future.

Action Item #7 – Keep a Positive Attitude in the Face of Failure

There is mountain here in Utah about 10-15 miles away from Salt Lake City called Pfeifferhorn. It is an 11,000 ft. triangular peak whose north ridge is really popular mountaineering route. When I first started mountaineering and rock climbing, my goal was to climb Pfeifferhorn. The pictures I saw of other climbers doing it were just amazing – the sheer cliffs, the incredible views, it was everything I wanted to have in an adventure.

So on my birthday in February, a couple of years back, I decided to go for it. I spent money on the equipment, training and the guide who would take me to my destination and guide me through the climb. One thing I didn't realize is the difficulty of the 4 hour ascent you need to do through waist high snow to get to the base of the ridge. I started snowshoeing with my guide at 5 AM.

As we climbed, I kept falling to the side and getting stuck in the snow, my feet and hands were starting to get extremely cold but I pushed on. By the time we got to the base of the ridge at just past 9 AM I had no energy left in me. On top of that, the gloves I had were too thin to allow me proper protection from absolutely biting cold at 10,000 feet in the middle of mountain wilderness.

There was no way for me to climb that peak. It would have been too dangerous for the condition I was in and I had no choice but to turn back. For a moment I felt humiliated and down-right depressed. Here I am, thinking I can conquer this mountain and instead I get my butt handed to me by Mother Nature. And to add insult to the injury, right on my birthday! But, as I talked to my guide, I started realizing that I am not the only person who called it quits and failed on this mountain before. Many climbers end up failing due to a lot of different factors, the weather might turn bad, they might not feel well, their equipment might fail. The important thing is to find a way to pick yourself up after this failure and come back at a later time.

In most things in life, whether in attraction, mountaineering or anything else, you will fail more times than you'll succeed. Failure is even more common when you're just learning a new skill. So how do you pick yourself up and keep going on? By expecting failure and accepting it as a normal way things work. It's just a side effect of a world that is completely out of your control.

Many men these days, in our culture of instant gratification, expect all things to work for them right from the start. When they're faced with failure, they get their will crushed and give up without ever trying again. As a result they never accomplish anything of significance and instead lead dull lives.

Failure, just like pain, is in fact good. It's a teacher of sorts and every time you experience it, it is a chance to learn a new lesson or repeat an old one until it truly sinks in. Look at some of the greatest minds in our history – Edison for example made 10,000 experiments before he came up with a light bulb. Another great example is the bestselling novel "The Help" written by Kathryn Stockett. The novel was rejected by 60 literary agents and each time the writer kept modifying and re-writing it, and then resubmitting it to be published. She even made changes to the novel as she was giving birth to her child. Now that's determination!

So expect failure, especially in the area of attraction. You might do everything just right but still fall flat on your face. Expect that to happen – I am now expecting most things in life not to work out for me from the first go. I found it better to get pleasantly surprised when things do work out than to have my hopes crushed when they don't.

Oh, and by the way, that day back in February, once we came down from the mountain, had a chance to eat lunch and thoroughly rest, my guide took me to this incredible 600 ft. frozen waterfall called Great White Icicle and taught me how to ice climb. Now, that was an awesome birthday present that I wouldn't have received had I just continued to stew in my disappointment.

Action Item #8 – Develop a Sense of Humor

This is a rally big thing. Women respond to a man who can make them laugh. It's an evolutionary response. Remember, the research has shown that men who can keep a sense of humor even in the toughest and most desperate situations, are the ones who have the best chance of survival. This makes sense - think about it, humor breaks up the tension and resets your mind away from desperation, panic and other negative emotions, and back into the survival mode.

Dating is also a form of a stressful situation. You see, we men are not the only ones who are nervous about interacting with opposite sex. Women are nervous too. They also have their own individual insecurities to worry about, but when you inject humor, especially the risqué kind, you release that tension and make her laugh even though she doesn't necessarily mean to.

How do you develop a sense of humor even if you are horrible at simple things like telling jokes? Practice – think of interesting or funny things that happened to you. What did you do? Who else was around? Describe the entire story in your head and then retell it over and over and each time try to improve it.

Add more details. Imagine your facial expression during that event and express it while telling the story. Then once you have it in your mind practice it in conversations with family and friends. See their reactions and adjust your story again to make it even funnier. Once you're satisfied with how it sounds, keep it in mind and use it at the appropriate moment when it's relevant to conversation.

Now, here is a really important trick to keep in mind. Use humor when interacting with women but don't overdo it. Keep a balance between your funny and your serious sides. Tell funny stories but try to add a serious note to them at the end. Also when you're discussing a serious topic, inject some humor at the right times. This switching back and forth between these two moods drives women wild.

Here's a really interesting thing that can explain why – researchers have found that woman prefer brooding men more during the time when they're ovulating. Brooding men are viewed as more of "alpha-male" types and appear more attractive for casual sex. However, their attractiveness falls as woman's cycle changes.

At the same time, women view men who are happy and smiling as more acceptable for long-term relationships and raising the family. They are generally looked at as being more submissive but also gentler and more likely to stay and help raise the children. So basically both types of men are attractive but for completely different reasons.

So when you combine your serious, brooding side, with your funny side and present them both at the same time, you're basically presenting to a woman best of both worlds. She sees your happy, gentler, more family oriented side while at the same time, she also sees the broodier, more masculine "alpha-male" side of your character. Basically, she's neither with immature clown nor with someone who's always in bad mood.

Like I said before – evolutionary jackpot.

Action Item #9 – Never Stop Learning

John Alanis has a really great saying – The school is never out for a pro. What this means is that no matter how knowledgeable you are, there is always more information out there that you could be learning, and ways that you could be improving your skill. Being a software developer by profession, I know first-hand how much people in my profession need to keep up with the latest technologies. Fail to learn anything new for a year and you're basically severely reducing your usefulness to your clients.

I always admired my mother in this regard. She a great example of someone who continuously strives to improve oneself. A pharmacist by profession, she came to this country at age 45 with neither a knowledge of English nor a diploma that's acceptable to American pharmacies (only American and Canadian diplomas can get you work in American pharmacies). Not having any of those things, she found work for a pharmaceutical company where she just sat on a production line and for a minimum wage monitored the line of medications the whole day for any defects.

At the same time she kept applying for a lab assistant position at the company research laboratory. Basically the lab assistant is a really fancy name for a dishwasher. Then one day all of a sudden she was laid off. Even though this was a major setback she still kept applying for lab position which she actually got few weeks later. That was all the opening in the door that she needed. While working as assistant she kept trying to help with experiments, something only scientists and lab technicians do. Outside of work hours she spent time studying English and slowly improving her writing and speaking skills, while at work she would stay extra hours just to get to work on new experiments and to learn how to operate the lab equipment.

Long story short, fast forward 15 years and not only did she become the lab technician, she is now a principal scientist in charge of all the senior scientists in her department. She is also the only principal scientist in the entire company (a Fortune 500 pharmaceutical corporation) that does not have a PhD! As a matter of fact, her expertise is so known and respected, she got a patent in her name approved few years back. And she accomplished all this by starting as a minimum-wage production line operator! She's now 60 years old but she still spends a few hours every day reading new research papers and researching new technologies.

Her example is what I always looked up to. No matter how much I learned about a certain subject, I always strived to learn more and to improve my skills. As a matter of fact, the more I learned about a certain subject the more I became aware of how little I knew about it. As with all things this also applies to the art of attraction. There are a lot of books, newsletters and other materials out there. So keep researching and reading about it. Even if the information is something you already know, at least now you got a confirmation from multiple sources that something truly works.

This process will also keep your mind fresh and engaged. A mind that's dormant is kind of like a still puddle of water – it eventually starts to stink. So keep learning and then start applying what you learned to the real life situations…

Action Item #10 – Practice, Practice, Practice

…Which brings us to this next action item. Everything that you learn needs to be tested in the real world. You can learn and read all you can about attraction but if you don't get out there and practice it repeatedly you will get nowhere and you'll still be where you are right now. Also, if you don't try using the information you just got, how will you know that what you've been taught really does work?

Attraction is a skill and just like any other skill it is learnable but only through applying what you learned in the real world. Skip that step and all you'll be is someone who can talk but can't perform.

There is an interesting book out there called Outliers by Malcolm Gladwell, I strongly suggest you read it. In it the author talks about the study that was done on concert violinists and their levels of mastery of the instrument. It turns out that the level of someone's skill in playing the violin or doing any other task, depends solely on the amount of time one spends practicing that skill. It's what's called "10,000 hour rule".

Basically, if you put 3 violinists together where the first one has an average skill, the second one is very good but not exceptional, and the third one who is a world-class master, and then compare their talents, abilities and the amount of time they spend practicing, the only significant variable that determines the level of expertise is the time spent practicing their skill. Any violinist who got to the master level of their art, practiced it more than 10,000 hours in their lifetime. It looks as if 10,000 hours is an actual tangible cutoff point at which the skill level of any person in any task reaches the master level. It means that anybody can achieve that level of mastery regardless of their talent if they apply themselves and practice long enough.

Think about it for a minute. This means that if you picked up a violin right now and started learning how to play and practiced 2-3 hours every single day for 365 days a year, in 9 to 13 years you too would be a world class master violinist! Now if that doesn't show you the untapped power of human abilities, I don't know what will!

In the same way, to just be good at something, a person needs to put in more than 3,000-4,000 hours practicing. Right there's your proof that if you want to get really, really good at art of attraction, you need to go out there in the real world and practice. So what does that mean?

Communicate with wide variety of women. Hang out and spend time with them and always try and show your attractive character and engage in attractive behaviors. Nothing beats that one-on-one feedback that you get from a real world interaction. You can use that to calibrate your approach and with each piece of positive or negative feedback apply some new type of action to get the results you want.

Action Item #11 – Use Social Proof to Your Advantage

When men judge the attractiveness of a woman, they always focus on physical characteristics. Basically we focus on physical features that we find attractive. What color of hair does she have, what is her shape, does she have large breasts, is she tall and slender? Depending on individual man's preferences, different physical features are more attractive than others,

Women also judge male appearance, but only as one of the indicators of his ability to produce healthy offspring and to protect and provide for her and her child. They look at your physical features as an indicator of higher testosterone levels which might mean that you are a strong, "alpha-male". The problem is that a lot of times these physical features are not accurate indicator of that ability. For example, I know quite a few people who look strong and ripped, but fall apart at the slightest sign of trouble.

So what other kinds of indicators can she use to determine if you are someone who is truly worthy of her attention? She can talk to you and get to know you to see if you have attractive traits and behaviors, but even that process is not a sure way to know – after all a guy who at first sight looks and behaves in the attractive manner, later turns out to be a "she man" in disguise.

So basically, women have no solid way to tell who is attractive and who is not – except by seeing how other women behave around a man and react to him. After all, what better way to tell someone's sexual worth than from the experience of other women? A recently done study has measured the level of attractiveness women felt toward different men based on their looks alone and then based on how other women reacted to the same men. They would show pictures of men with different body shapes and sizes standing by themselves and asked them to rate their attractiveness. Then they would show the same women pictures of same individuals with women either smiling or frowning at them. The men who in previous round were not found highly attractive were viewed much more favorably when displayed with a woman that was smiling and enjoying their company.

The findings confirm that the way other women behave toward a man has more of an effect on how other women perceive his level of attractiveness. So how can you use this to your own advantage? Well, let me ask you – do you have any good female friends? If, hopefully, you do, then use them as your wingmen – hang out with them in public and just have fun. Then while you are in their company, approach other women and start the conversations where you display your attractive character. Other women will notice you already hanging out with another woman or women and will give you a benefit of a doubt that you would not have if you were only with your male friends or alone. It's basically a way to give yourself "social proof".

And "social proof" is extremely effective tool – it lets women know that you have already been vetted by another woman and that you have already passed all of their "tests". You therefore must be an attractive character and someone worth investing time in.

Action Item #12 – Bring Out a Bad Girl in Her

You know that old song – "It's a Man's Man's Man's World" by James Brown? What it says in the refrain is quite accurate:

"This is a man's world, this is a man's world
But it wouldn't be nothing, nothing without a woman or a girl…"

Since the dawn of our society men had strong tendencies to control the behavior of women and their sexuality. Women have throughout the history been relegated to the status of second-class citizens. With few famous exceptions, they were not trusted to have education, to govern, take care of business, or later on in history, to vote. And even though today we live in more egalitarian society, there is still a tremendous amount of pressure on women to present themselves and behave in certain ways.

Basically, the society is still not allowing women to fully express themselves and to be who they are. Many women hide their sexual sides from public view so as to avoid harsh judgment of others, while we guys get a much more lenient treatment. Think about what are some of the names given to women who dare to expose their natural sexual tendencies. I'm not going to write them here since I never call women these names and I also don't hang around guys who do. But you get an idea.

So what happens to a woman who wants to have a successful career and a solid standing in a society where she is respected and admired – she is forced to hide her "naughty-girl" side. Otherwise she stands a real chance of damaging her reputation and destroying all the hard work she put in building her career.

Women silently resent this! Think about it - men don't have to worry about this as much. Even when we guys do get caught with our pants down, the consequences are not as severe as in the case of women. What would have happened if instead of Bill Clinton, it was Hilary standing in front of the camera as a president saying that she did indeed have an inappropriate relationship "with that man"? I don't care what your political leanings are, I bet you anything she would have been forced to resign.

So like any other person, who has to hide their true nature, women appreciate it when they feel safe in the environment in which they can express their true self. And if you as a man can create that environment, you become a rare commodity in their eyes.

Here's an example of a little social experiment I did in turning a group of women I just met into a bunch of laughing, bad girls who were having all kinds of sexy, naughty fun with me. I was invited to wine tasting party by a friend. This was my first wine testing party since I'm more of a beer guy, and I didn't know anybody at that place other than the friend that invited me. The theme of the party was Spanish wines – the topic an average chimp would know more about than I do.

So I come over and introduce myself to various people at the party. There were many different individuals at the place including some very hot women. The women were all dressed nice and most of them had high-level careers. Some were doctors, managers, nurses, office workers and etc. Like with any party people tend to gravitate towards small groups and this was no exception. The conversation was polite and kind of subdued since most people didn't know others at the party.

At that point I kind of gave a challenge to myself to see how quickly I could take a conversation with a group of women (and with a little help of alcohol) to a very naughty place, and how long would it take me to get these, otherwise very proper and professional looking women, to start showing their bad girl sides.

So I approach a group of 3 very hot women and 2 "she men". I introduce myself and join the conversation. I silently promised myself ahead of time that I will not put any topic off limits no matter how awkward of a response I get back from my group. So we start talking and as the conversation goes on I start introducing little by little, sexual innuendo into our topics. As I'm doing that I start telling funny stories and jokes about male sexual organs, our performance anxieties, what women think of us guys in bed, all the while challenging them to come up with their similar stories. The ears of all the women in the group perk up while at the same time, the 2 guys are starting to get a bit uncomfortable, probably thinking that something very inappropriate is about to happen.

Next thing I know, the women in the group, very coyly move the conversation and jokes from generic male sexual organs to my sexual organs. And then to the size and shape of my penis, the size of my butt, the hairiness of my body all while I'm telling jokes laced with sexual innuendo. Now the girls are all laughing hysterically, talking loud, having fun with me and starting to touch me all over to confirm for themselves that what I'm saying about my physical attributes is true. Yes, I'm hairy, yes my butt is really small and no, they can't touch anywhere else, which in other words means that they will try and touch everywhere else. In the meantime, the "she men" in the group are also laughing but at a much lower volume and are pretty much eclipsed out of the conversation. The focus of all the women in the group is now on me and I'm the beneficiary of all their attention.

One of the ladies that was listening to our conversation from outside of our group, all of a sudden stepped in and told me flat out that she would never grab my butt nor any other man's even if she was crazy about me. I simply responded that she will not know what she truly likes if she does not get out of her shell and experience other, finer, things in life. I told her to seize the day – "Carpe Diem" or in this case "Carpe Ass-em" to which she started laughing. And guess what, it didn't take much for her to really seize the opportunity!

So, there is an example of a group of high-level, professional women, at an event that's meant to be about wine tasting and just casual conversation (and really when I think of wine tasting, the word "snob" always comes to mind), who at the first chance and with a right approach turn into a pack of out of control naughty girls. I'm sure these women came to that same party thinking that it was going to be a boring, snobbish affair, and yet, they had a really great fun time that they can tell their girlfriends about and have even more laughs.

And it was really easy to get them to behave that way. The point is – if I could do it any man can do it too! It takes some time and practice but in the end women will greatly appreciate it. First don't treat them as if they are some precious, sensitive beings that you have to walk around on shells. They are not – they're human beings just like you and I.

Second, have a conversation with them but then slowly add some sexual innuendo to it and steer the topic toward more naughty subjects. Keep in mind that some women don't like profanity in which case I use medical terms if I talk about male or female sex organs or sexual acts. If I hear her use a profanity then I'm ok to use it myself. You don't have to use profane language to have a naughty conversation – as a matter of fact in some cases, not using that language will make you look more intelligent and exciting.

Third – don't shy away from any topics. Nothing is really out of bounds but only if you can make an intelligent and funny observation about it. The point is not to take a topic and make a vulgar, simple-minded comment about it aiming for cheap laughs. You will only lose people's respect which will in turn cause them to leave you.

And finally – include them and encourage them to take it to the next level. The point is not only to talk about it yourself. The point is to have them not only talk about it, but also actively act in a naughty and sexy way. Challenge them, tease them, dare them to do things. Have them touch you or allow you to touch them.

The point is, you will stick out in their mind as a different and exciting man, a man around whom they can truly be safe and express their sexual character. So when a time comes that you are with them in a more intimate setting, it will be much easier for you to close the deal. And that is a really, really good thing!

Action Item #13 – Close the Deal

In this entire book, I have tried to not only show you and give you real-life examples of attractive behaviors, but to also get you to act on what you have learned. After all, you don't know for sure if what I'm telling you is correct or not, until you try it out. And one of the most important actions you'll need to take is to have her sleep with you. That is the whole point of what we're trying to accomplish here. If you don't make your move then all of what we discussed above is pointless.

You might be nervous about figuring out the right time to take the action and close the deal. You might want to wait until the right time presents itself, but when exactly is the right time? First of all, you will never be able to tell the right time with absolute certainty. Unless you can read her mind, you will not know for sure when she's ready. However, some specific body language can be a good indicator that she's ready for you to make the move. Is she smiling at you flirtatiously and moving her body closer to you? Is she touching you often? While doing all of that does she also bite her lips or play with her hair? All of these could be indicators that you should man up and go for it, but the truth is no matter how much you observe and analyze, you will not know for sure unless you try it.

Another fear that often stops the guys dead in their tracks is the fear that they will not be able to sexually satisfy her. We psych ourselves out, and it gets even worse the more we like the girl that we are with. Look, it's fine; we've all been there. I've been there myself more times than I would like to admit and yet I have never, ever, ever been dumped by the girl for not being able to perform on our first time. Anyone who is telling you that she'll dump you or humiliate you if you don't perform is either lying or trying to sell you a penis enlargement pill. Don't believe it for a second.

I had so many friends call me and ask me for advice about how to deal with this issue. And they range from 21 year old ripped rock climber, to an amateur body builder in his mid-20's, and from guys in mid-30's all the way to men in their 60's. The key each time is to realize that this sometimes happens and it's normal. Trust me in that situation, women are often blaming themselves just as much as you do. Their insecurities kick in too. They might feel like their bodies are not attractive enough for you.

If you're lucky enough to be with a more experienced woman, then it's even less of an issue. She's probably seen this more than once and will just try and pillow talk to you and try to make you more comfortable, but like I said, I've never had nor have I ever heard of any of men that I know that have been dumped by a women because this issue has happened to them.

The worst possible thing you can do in a situation like this is to make a scene out of it. For that she will probably kick you out of her life. First time performance issue are not an indicator of your current or future sexual prowess but your lousy attitude and childish behavior certainly are.

So get it out of your heads and stop psyching yourselves out. Trust me, you'll be fine. And in the off chance (no matter how small that chance is) that you do get dumped because of it, don't take it as your personal failure. Think of that woman as of someone you would not want to be with anyways. If she's that high maintenance that even the slightest problem causes her to leave you, what would happen if you are together when something more serious occurs? You wouldn't want people like her around you if you ever find yourself in real trouble.

Go To:
www.EffortlessCommunication.com/dj to Access Your Bonus Videos and Mystery Gift

Section 4: How to Avoid the Pitfalls That Kill Attraction

Avoiding the Dangers

We have covered a lot of stuff and I hope you now have a solid plan on what to do to start attracting beautiful women. But keep in mind that through this process of learning, you need to be careful to avoid making some very serious mistakes. These are not just simple learning curve screw-ups where you say or do something to destroy the attraction that you built with a woman. Those mistakes you can recover from easily and continue on. No, these are more serious mistakes that could keep you permanently stuck in the unattractive category or worse, haunt you for the rest of your life.

I have listed some of the most common pitfalls that we guys fall into when we first start attracting women. I have also explained the dangers that can arise from making these mistakes. You can basically divide them into two categories, mistakes that affect your life, and the ones that affect the opinion and view people have of you. Both can be very damaging and affect other areas of your life and not just your relationships.

Dangerous Pitfall #1 – Comparing Yourself to Others

In my opinion this is one of the most poisonous attitudes a man can have – constantly measuring himself against the others. It stinks of jealousy, immaturity and desperation. It also gets you nowhere in your life. Yes, you might push yourself harder to achieve success but you will also take failures and setbacks with much more pain and disappointment than you normally would with a healthy attitude. And then you run the risk of taking this pain and disappointment and acting out on it in your relationship.

Constantly pushing yourself just to outdo the next person does not allow you to properly enjoy your successes and brings you little joy in life in general. Listen, there are over 7 billion people in this world and no matter how good you are at something or other, how successful you are or how much your skills improve, there will always be somebody out there who is better, smarter or more successful than you. You can't beat them all.

I remember reading an article in Forbes magazine about their "Richest People in the World" list and the Saudi billionaire Prince al-Waleed bin Talal. You might have heard of the guy – he is one of the world's richest investors and he recently purchased his own customized Airbus A-380 double-decker plane for over $300M. Forbes writers and editors accused him of calling them, pleading, threatening and crying (yes, actually crying on the phone!) because – wait for it – they moved him down few spots on the list of richest people in the world! Here is a highly successful man, at the top of the %0.0001 of the world's wealthiest people behaving like a total immature child, throwing tantrums when he feels outdone by others. Now think about what that kind of behavior does to his level of attractiveness to women. What does it say about his character and his level of respect for others? Yes, he's super-rich but no self-respecting woman would hang around this whiner even if he does have his own flying palace.

Avoiding this kind of behavior is especially important in the area of attraction. You might be successful with women but if you see a friend with a beautiful girlfriend and you get jealous, not only will you lose your friend's respect, but also the respect of his girlfriend and any other woman that she associates with.

What you're doing with your envy and jealousy is robbing the people around you of your appreciation of their success. Most people want to be recognized for their achievements. They want to earn your respect by showing you their success. Basically when they show you their achievements, what they are really telling you is that you are important enough to them that they want your admiration and congratulation. It's a great type of compliment. Why display envy and ruin their enjoyment of success? If the roles were reversed wouldn't you want to feel appreciated and admired?

So avoid this type of behavior at all costs and focus instead on what you consider to be your success. Did you do the best you can to get where you are? Did you accomplish the goals you set out for yourself even if those goals are not as lofty as owning your own plane? If the answer is yes to all of the above, than there's the reason enough to be satisfied and proud of your accomplishments.

Dangerous Pitfall #2 –Putting Her on a Pedestal

Some of you might be reading this because you are interested in attracting one specific girl, maybe somebody who's been an object of your affection for a while but who you haven't been able to close. Nothing wrong with that but I have one suggestion for you - unless you're trying to date Queen of England, she has no place being put on a pedestal. Look, I know that you are attracted to her and she probably is a really great and attractive girl, but keep in mind that she's just a human being like any other. The sun does not rise and set between her breast and butt cheeks.

If you learned anything from the example of Don Juan, it's that attracting by not trying to attract is the best course of action. No matter what you learn in here, if you don't get rid of that feeling of being smitten by her, you will not improve your skills. The best thing you might do is to quit hanging around her for a while and instead focus on learning these skills by interacting with other women.

This will do two things for you – it will make you aware of the fact that there are other women out there, some of which are just as much or even more attractive than she is. And second, your separation will stop the effect that she has on you – next time you see her after you get better in the skill of attraction, you will be able to pursue her with a clearer and calmer head - that is if you haven't already decided that there are other, better fish in the sea.

Dangerous Pitfall #3 – Disregarding the Reality

When I first started learning to fly a plane, one of the things that made me kind of shell shocked was the sheer amount of controls and gages. The plane is nothing like a car – with a car you have a steering wheel, gas pedal, clutch and a break. On your dashboard, you have fuel, engine temperature, RPM and speed gages and that's it.

In a plane you have a flight control stick in your hands, rudder control at your feet, the brake pedals right above the rudder control, the separate throttle and fuel mixture controls, magneto switch, fuel line cut of switch, circuit breakers, as well as fuel gage, air speed indicator, the vertical speed indicator, artificial horizon, altimeter and on and on and on... And don't get me even started on the radio communication controls. And this is just on a small single-engine two-seater Cessna 152. It was enough to get my head spinning before we even took off for the first time.

You have to be so aware of all of your gages and controls at all times since any of those could indicate a potentially serious problem. You can't just focus on one thing even though it is so tempting to do. For example, I always tended to focus on my air speed since that's basically the difference between flying and falling. In my focus on air speed, as I would make a turn I used to inadvertently press rudder too hard when there was no need to, jerking the plane to the side. I got my flight instructor PO-ed at me a few times for doing that.

I understood then and there why some pilots crash their planes in what FAA calls "controlled flight into terrain". In a nutshell what that term means is that the pilot focuses on one or couple of controls so much that they disregard all other inputs and fail to notice that they are actually flying into the ground while still being fully in control of the aircraft.

Attraction is just like that. It is the feeling that tends to take over all of your senses so much that you are literally flying blind without really losing control. You focus on the good feeling so much that you fail to notice some really questionable behaviors or tendencies of your date. You either plain out don't notice them or you justify them. Anything to get the party going and to keep the feeling of attraction alive.

The problem is that those kinds of justifications are masking something that could be a serious issue later down the line. Again, at the extreme end, think of Jodi Arias example. I'm sure she displayed some disturbing tendencies before going and full out murdering her boyfriend. It makes me wonder if he noticed any of them and if he justified them in some way.

So enjoy the feeling of attraction but make sure you keep one eye on the reality around you. Just like a pilot who is aware of all of his surroundings, your vigilance in the process of attraction might just keep you out of a news story where a three-letter federal agency is trying to investigate the cause of your demise.

Dangerous Pitfall #4 – Sharing Your Personal Problems

Life isn't fair. You might be going through a hard time in your life. Maybe you got sick or went through a divorce, or maybe you lost your job. It's not fair, it sucks, but it is your reality. It, however, is not the reality of the woman you're interacting with. She has her own problems to deal with and the only thing she wants from you is fun time and the feeling of attraction.

The hard truth is that your worth to other people goes only as far as the benefits that you provide to them. When those benefits are gone, so is your usefulness. If you think that by talking about your problems and hardships you're going to get someone who just met you and who's just getting to know you, to take pity on you, you're sorely mistaken. Again, put yourself in their position - You wouldn't tolerate a moody or sad person in your company, especially when your goal at the moment is to have fun.

This doesn't mean that your troubles and hardships are not relevant, it just means that they are only important to you and not to somebody who is just barely getting to know you. So if your state of mind is so preoccupied with your issues that you can't focus on creating attraction with women, do yourself a favor and stay at home and work through them. Don't try to drag others into it, especially not a woman who you just met and are trying to attract. You are not her child and she is not your mommy that will be there to kiss away your boo-boos.

As a result of behaving in this way you will appear to her as moody, week, boring and not somebody who she would want to be around. Once you manage to solve your problems, then get back into the game and start fresh. You need to show yourself as a strong, reliable man, someone who demands and deserves her respect. This is the only way to get her to respond to you and truly like you.

Leave the moping and moaning to lesser men, ones that will never truly understand women or be respected by them.

Dangerous Pitfall #5 – Not Caring About Your Reputation

Your reputation is simply how other people see you. Think about it – if I were to ask you right now what your reputation is would you have an answer? If you haven't thought about it, you probably don't know. And yet, it is one of the single most important factors that determines how successful you're going to be with women.

Let's use an analogy – just like business uses advertising and sales people to get customers to buy their products, you use your attraction skills to get women to buy into you and your abilities to both satisfy them physically and emotionally. Yet no amount of advertising and sales skill is going to help you if the word gets out that you or your product sucks. You can play "bad boy" all you want but if women spread damaging stories about you, you're done for.

Let me just give you an example of how not managing my reputation got me in trouble in my first business. I used to own a small fitness club with my partner, ethnic Armenian who grew up in former Soviet Union. Our club thrived at first, but just like most other small businesses we did not think hard enough about our potential vulnerabilities and were in return pummeled by the last recession. Still, my partner and I persevered while pretty much every other club in a 5-mile range around us either got sold off or closed its doors.

Just at those critical moments as we were trying to keep our heads above the water, we noticed that some of our most important clients started mysteriously canceling their memberships without giving us any reason why. We wondered if we did something to upset them, if our customer service was to blame or if the operating hours of our facility were inconvenient, or if our pricing structure was not competitive, but nothing was coming up as an obvious red flag. Then one day a friend of mine and a fellow business owner down the street from us, told me he overheard people in a local restaurant talking and spreading rumors how my fitness club is a cover for Russian mob's money laundering operation!

Apparently, someone started this really vicious rumor, maybe a competitor who went out of business or somebody else, but either way, it was out there and circulating! Apparently, my partner's Eastern European heritage, his accent and the fact that his skin was darker, and that he was really muscular and buff was all it took for people to believe in this lie. It didn't matter that he is one of the nicest, most polite people you'll ever meet or that he would bend over backwards to help any client. Never in the million years in my naïve thinking would I have come up with something like this as being a reason why we were losing clients.

So, just like the above example, if you don't actively think how you are viewed by people around you, no amount of attractive behavior is going to help you – you'll still be going home alone. Now – what's the easiest way to maintain your reputation? Be true to who you are. That's it – as simple as that.

Let me give you an example – when we guys think of an attractive characters, one of the first ones that comes to mind is James Bond, especially when played by Daniel Craig. He is extremely fit, skilled at fighting and driving fast cars, is not afraid to get in all kinds of dangers or take on any kind of a bad guy. He has a serious demeanor that hides a quick mind and a great sense of humor. The pitfall is, while most of us men, would love to be as attractive as James Bond, very few of us have the skills to pull of things that he does. In my entire life I've met only one man who could pull that off and he was trained for many years by U.S. government and has been in many of the world's most dangerous places.

So, let me ask you – what do you think happens to a regular guy who tries to act as James Bond without skills to match? Eventually, he comes into a situation where his words and his reality end up clashing. Maybe he crosses paths with a dude who is really skilled at fighting and gets his butt kicked. Or maybe he goes to a gun shooting range and accidentally shoots off his big toe.

Either way, once he is exposed for his lack of skill and shown as a fake, the story of that event then gets to propagate, because there are very few things people like to do more in this day and age than talk about embarrassments and failures of others. So once these stories start circulating, what do you think happens to the poor guy if he approaches another woman with his James Bond shtick? He gets laughed out of course. And even if he never tries that approach again, the damage is done – he's already a laughing stock.

The truth is, you don't have to be James Bond to be attractive. You do however need to know what your personal strengths and weaknesses are and adjust your behavior such that your weaknesses are not shown while your positive strengths are stressed. This doesn't mean that you shouldn't work on improving your weak spots, it just means that you should not present yourself as someone you're not.

Now, even if you do all of these things, you might end up in a situation where to no fault of your own, someone starts spreading damaging rumors and false stories about you. How do you deal with the damage that's caused by it? Well, first you have to know that there's a rumor circulating to begin with. For that you have to rely on trusted friends in your circle. They are the first ones that will come to you (if they're truly your friends) and let you know about it.

Then, once you become aware of it, you need to squash it. The only method that ever worked for me is to confront the rumors head on. Don't' hide away from them, don't try to avoid them – instead talk to other people about them. Let it be the first thing you mention when you see someone you know and then just let them know how incredibly ridiculous that rumor is and why.

Back to the example with my business – right away, to confront the Russian mob rumor, I went on Facebook and let everybody know what I heard and what is circulating around. I also had a weekly newsletter that I used to send to all our club clients. I sent an emergency issue directly stating what happened and stating in plain language why this rumor was false. I also offered any client full refund of their last month's membership fee and cancelation of their contract if they did not want to do business with us because of what I just disclosed. Not only did we not lose any clients, we had many of them respond back to us giving us their support.

Dangerous Pitfall #6 – Thinking that Attraction Will Last Forever

As you get better at attracting women, you will undoubtedly come across a girl that you feel strong attraction to, who in fact is attracted back to you. It is a great feeling, especially if up to that point you couldn't attract a woman like that. It is very easy to get lost in that feeling, and even easier to believe in a myth that this feeling will last forever.

Our society teaches us that the only true way to go forward in your relationship when these feelings are present is to get married. Marriage is presented as this state of bliss where two souls finally get to join each other and live happily ever after. Do not believe this lie and don't jump head-first into marriage!

In real world marriage is nothing close to that. Marriage is a hard work where two people have to constantly negotiate on their differences and meet each other's expectations. The challenge also increases as time goes by and our habits, preferences and views change. If anything, marriage might end up being an antidote to the initial feelings of attraction. Just see how Byron describes marriage in Don Juan:

"Marriage from love, like vinegar from wine –
    A sad, sour sober beverage – by time

Is sharpen'd from its high celestial flavor
Down to a very homely household savor."

Like "vinegar from wine" – what a great and accurate metaphor. Now don't get me wrong, marriage is not a bad thing. Vinegar is not wine but its flavor still has place at the table and can be quite enjoyable in a different context. Marriage can be a great experience but like I said above, it takes hard work and commitment from both parties. If either you or her are not willing to put in that commitment, your marriage will certainly fail.

The initial feelings of attraction will eventually fade and if you get caught in a trap of marriage without truly thinking if the person you married is committed to you, then you are about to be in a lot of pain. The stress from divorce is often compared to having a loved one die. It's an appropriate comparison since you are in fact losing a loved one. They just get to go on living without you. All of your initial hopes and dreams of future get shattered by cruel reality and you are left with some very real emotional and financial consequences.

So avoid this trap at all cost and think outside of the feeling of attraction. Try to consider who your partner really is and gage her ability to commit to you. For example, some ways to judge her commitment to you is to see if she keeps her word to you. Also, does she take a good care of herself and her environment? If she does, then she most likely will take care of the environment that both of you are in.

What kinds of accomplishments does she have? Did she accomplish something that took a long time to do like getting a college degree or a promotion at her job? Or does she give up on her goals or tasks easily, at the first sign of a problem? If she gives up easily on herself, what do you think the chances are that she's going to bail out on your marriage when trouble times hit.

Is she lazy or does she work hard toward her goals? Does she even have any aspirations in her life or is she going aimlessly through it? People who don't have any goals or aspirations tend to have a lot more free time on their hands and are easily bored. Will she then rely on you to be the escape from her boredom? When you go after your goals and are not around to entertain her, will she find some other man to help her escape her boredom?

Think through the answers to all of the above questions and if those answer point to this woman not being a marriage material, then make sure that the extent of your relationship ends at casual dating.

Conclusion

Don Juan is a great character and you should read Byron's work. Even though it was written at the start of 19th century, it's relevant to our age especially because there is so much nonsense now propagated in media and Hollywood about how relationships and attraction "should work".

But don't just stop at reading – my hope is that now, through the action strategies I showed, you actually are motivated and have fire in your belly to really make positive changes in your life. Keep in mind though that there are those major mistakes that we also discussed and avoid making them at all cost.

So read, learn, practice and act. Then maybe one day, a famous writer just might make a book about your adventures.

Good luck!

Go To:
www.EffortlessCommunication.com/dj to
Access Your Bonus Videos and Mystery
Gift

MORE Important Titles by John Alanis

Women Approach You Series Volume 4:
How to Make Women CRAVE You
http://amzn.to/TwnyYd

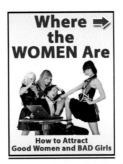

Women Approach You Series Volume 5:
Where the WOMEN Are: How to Attract Good Women and BAD
Girls
http://amzn.to/12nPB1o

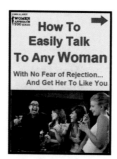

Women Approach You Series Volume 6:
How To Easily Talk To Any Woman, Without Fear Of Rejection
And Get Her To Like You Too
http://amzn.to/Uoco7I

Click Here For John's Complete Catalog of Books:

http://www.effortlesscommunication.com/amazon/complete-catalog.htm

Made in the USA
Monee, IL
05 July 2021